THE BENIDORM BOOZER'S BIBLE

THE A-Z OF SPANISH BOOZE

HANGOVER CURES

HOW TO GET OFF THE BEACH AND INTO THE PUB

CARTOONS, QUOTES & QUIZZES

THINGS THAT ARE DIFFICULT TO SAY WHEN YOU'RE DRUNK

Innovative

Cinnamon

Edward Woodward

THINGS THAT ARE VERY DIFFICULT TO SAY WHEN YOU'RE DRUNK

Specificity

British Constitution

Ken Dodd's Dad's Dog's Dead

THINGS THAT ARE IMPOSSIBLE TO SAY WHEN YOU'RE DRUNK

Thanks, but I don't want to have sex.

Nope, no more booze for me.

Sorry, but you're not really my type.

Good evening officer, isn't it lovely out tonight?

Oh, I couldn't, nobody wants to hear me sing.

THE BENIDORM BOOZER'S BIBLE

DRINKING THE SPANISH WAY

Welcome to the Benidorm Boozer's Bible. There is a way to enjoy drinking in Spain and it is linked to eating. A beer, sherry or vermouth with 'tapas' before lunch. Wine, and plenty of it, with lunch. A glass of Licor de Hierbas after lunch. All followed by a good over-the-table session (sobremesa) before a siesta that gets you back in shape for a great night out.

THE A-Z OF SPANISH BOOZE

Coming up is an A-Z of the best drinks you can try in Spain.

One word of warning: In terms of quality you get what you pay for, in terms of quantity you get what you deserve (and don't forget to book that taxi back to the hotel).

But first, a toast.

¡ARRIBA,
ABAJO,
AL CENTRO
Y ADENTRO!

This Spanish toast is celebrated by everyone around the table. Each person holds up their drink and chants out aloud, moving their glass as follows:

UP! DOWN!
TO THE CENTRE!
(OF THE TABLE)
DOWN THE HATCH!

AGUARDIENTE / ORUJO

Eau de Vie or Aqua Vitae. The Arab secret of distilling wine passed to Spain 800 years ago. The best is made on smallholdings in Galicia known as 'Orujo'. On St. James's day (Santiago), look out for Quemada, a flaming cauldron that will blow your head off. It's made using 4 bottles of Orujo, 1kg of sugar, coffee beans & lemon peel, stirred and boiled for 15 minutes. To make spiced Orujo, buy a bottle of the pure stuff and add 3 sprigs of thyme, rosemary and savory, 1 sprig of lemon verbena, 6 sage leaves, 6 mint leaves, 2 cups of dry anís, 2 cups of sweet anís, and the peel of half an orange cut into strips. Knock out!

ANÍS

The brand of anís each Spaniard drinks is a very personal choice. It tastes like Pernod and is distilled from aniseed which comes from the family of herbs we call dill.

If you like your Spanish anís sweet, try 'La Castellana dulce'. If you prefer the stronger, dry anis, go for 'Chinchón seco'. Anís also comes lemon flavoured and there is a herb flavoured version from Ibiza called 'Hierbas Ibicencas'.

THE THINGS THEY SAY

"Benidorm's ours! The Spanish can have Blackpool!"

Comedian Rikki Stevens

BOTELLÍN

Originally describing a small carafe of wine, a botellín (pronounced 'bot-te-yin'), is now exclusively used to ask for a small 20cl bottle of beer.

This is a somewhat paltry amount of beer to English eyes, but as beer quickly warms up in the Spanish summer heat, it should be seen as a quick, refreshing glug to quench the thirst. A 33cl bottle is called a 'Tercio' (pronounced 'terthy-o').

CAÑA

A caña (pronounced 'can-ya') is a lash of beer to calm your nerves. That is, a small glass of ice-cold draft beer served from the tap.

Going back a few years it was sometimes given to children (presumably to calm their nerves!).

If you want a bigger glass ask for 'una caña doble' (a double) or 'una jarra de cerveza' (a pint of beer).

CARAJILLO

The word comes from the Spanish word for 'courage'. When the Spanish army invaded Cuba they would shout the rallying cry, "¡Vamos a coger corajillo!". Battle over, they would retire to the bar and ask for a 'Carajillo' or coffee with a shot of Cuban rum in it.

Nowadays, it is a freshly brewed cup of strong coffee with a brandy in it. Add powdered cinnamon and sugar to taste.

CAVA

Bubbly cava is produced using the same method as champagne and is the world's best-selling sparkling wine. Cava ranges from Dulce (sweet) to Extra Brut (extra dry) which refers to the amount of sugar in it.

The most popular are Semi-seco and Brut from the Freixinet and Cordoniu wineries in Sant Sadurní d'Anoia in Catalonia. Cava Gran Reserva is cava that has been aged for at least 30 months in the bottle.

CERVEZA RUBIA

What we call Lager. San Miguel or Amstel may be what you're used to asking for in Spanish bars. The 5 star red & gold Mahou (pronounced "Ma-oo") is better and doesn't go flat like the 'classic' green & gold Mahou.

If you like your beer with extra fizz try Cruzcampo. Estrella Damm from Catalonia is also worth a try as is Estrella Galicia. This is good on tap when served from gravity fed copper tanks that hang high over the taps so there's no need to add extra gas to get it to the pump.

THE THINGS THEY SAY

"One beer's too many, ten's not enough"

Ex-England football great, Paul Gascoigne.

CERVEZA NEGRA

Brown beers are brown because they're made using caramelised sugar. Spanish dark beers taste a bit like Brown Ale but are fizzy like lager. Mahou do a black beer (cerveza negra) but VollDamm from the Estrella Damm stable has more taste.

Spanish dark beers have nothing like the class of British beers and are inferior to foreign export beers, especially Belgian beers.

CHUPITO

A chupito is a shot glass of licor. It is often taken after a meal around the table as a toast and digestif.

Unless you ask for your favorite tipple, you will most likely be given Orujo "blanco" (clear) or "con hierbas" (yellow).

The normal Spanish measure for a glass of licor is about three times that in the UK, so if you only want a taste at a third of the price, ask for a chupito.

COGNAC

Oddly, if you want to drink Spanish brandy in a Spanish bar or restaurant, you must ask for a 'Cognac', then select the label of your choice.

Spanish brandies are darker in colour and stronger tasting than French brandies but stand up well to comparison. Try Magno or Torres 10.

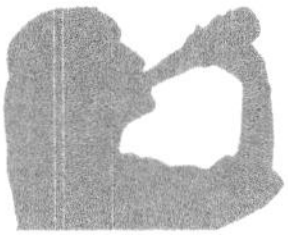

Ask Beni: Keep a bottle of water by your bed, not a glass, it's easier for your lips to latch onto in the dark.

DYC

Pronounced 'dick', Dyc was the first whisky to be produced in Spain. It is distilled in Segovia and there are three varieties.

The 3-year old whisky is cheap and should be drunk with mixers. The 8-year old variety, known as Dyc Ocho, is fine on the rocks.

Dyc Pure Malt is made using water from the River Eresma in a traditional process dating back to 1959.

GIN AND TONIC

The way to ask for a gin and tonic is as one word and as fast as you can - 'Jintonik' - like an Oriental who is about to miss a train and needs a ticket fast.

The Spanish use plenty of gin which is as it should be. There are a myriad of flavours and added spices on the market. It all depends on your preference and your budget.

3 parts gin

5 parts tonic water

Wedge of lime (or lemon)

HOLIDAY BOOK

"His hand desperately clutching a bottle of stout, he kissed Mary's feverish mouth and she opened his shirt and kissed his chest. Rolling around with the flesh of it... My problems come with me wherever I go, even on detours."

'The Ginger Man' by J. P. Donleavy

(extract)

JEREZ

I used to associate sherry with my gran at Christmas, but it's a drink full of flavour and class. The word Sherry comes from the Spanish word "Jerez". Jerez de la Frontera in Andalusia is the home of Sherry.

Sherry is made from wines further matured by ageing in barrels made of Canadian white oak and is usually drunk as an appetizer. There are three basic varieties, Dry, Medium and Cream but the flavours are so subtle that they are subdivided again.

DRY & MEDIUM SHERRY

The most popular is Fino, often called 'Vino Fino' as it is drunk as wine in Andalusia. It is a pale, golden sherry with a sharp bouquet.

Manzanilla is a more refined dry sherry. Amontillado, originally from Montilla is an amber coloured, medium sherry.

Palo Cortado is a sherry with a persistent flavour that falls between Amontillado and the sweet sherry known as Oloroso.

SWEET SHERRY

Sweet sherry is dry sherry blended with sweet wine. Pale Cream sherry is a golden dry Fino to which sweet wine-must is added to make it sweet.

Oloroso is a mahogany coloured nutty medium, sweet sherry and Moscatel is a sweet, dark mahogany coloured sherry produced from the Muscat grape.

If you like a really rich, raisin-sweet sherry try Pedro Ximénez.

YOUR ROUND / MY ROUND: STATS

TRUE OR FALSE:
There are 10,500 light bulbs along
Benidorm's beach fronts.

TRUE OR FALSE:
At 55 storeys, the Hotel Bali, Benidorm
is Europe's highest.

TRUE OR FALSE:
There are 201 rubbish bins on Benidorm's
Poniente and Levante beaches.

(ANSWERS P79)

KALIMOTXO

Pronounced 'Kalimocho' this is a popular drink among the young, and the peculiar spelling comes from the Basque country. It's not much of a cocktail as it is just a 50/50 mix of Cola and red wine.

Kalimotxo is often drunk by the litre at all night gatherings, known as a Botellones, in local parks or town squares. These have been officially banned on grounds of noise, litter and the morning-after smell in nearby streets, but that's not going to stop the young .having a good time.

THE THINGS THEY SAY

"Fat, drunk, and stupid is
no way to go through life, son."

Dean Wormer, (Animal House).

LICOR 43

Licor Cuarenta y Tres evolved from a thousand-year-old secret Arabic formula that blends 43 natural ingredients. Most of these are fruits and fragrant herbs, so it is a drink quite different from any other.

Licor Cuarenta y Tres is 31 percent proof, so less strong than a normal spirit but well worth trying on the rocks. It can also be mixed with chocolate and vanilla for a really sweet cocktail, or with lime juice if you prefer sour flavours. Better quality than Alcopops.

LOTERIA NACIONAL

Fancy buying a lottery ticket? Tickets for the National Lottery are sold each week. What you buy is a fraction of a 5 figure number (eg a 10th part of number such as 20957). The price is on the ticket. Look for the draw in Saturday's newspaper. If the last figure (7) matches that on the winning number you get a free ticket. If the last 3 figures match (957) you win your tenth part of the listed prize money. If all five match, break open the champagne. Cash in your winning ticket at the local lottery office.

MANZANILLA

A refined, dry sherry that deserves a page of its own. Manzanilla comes from Sanlúcar de Barrameda in Andalusia. Light on the palate and drunk ice-cold on a warm summer's day, it's a marvellous aperitif with shrimp or prawns.

If you ask for it, make sure the restaurant doesn't serve you a cup of Camomile tea because it has exactly the same name.

MID-AFTERNOON COCKTAIL

In 1795, a New Orleans' chemist first mixed brandy toddies with his own bitters and served them in an egg-cup. The drink took the name of the cup, in English "cocktay". Try this one.

Cranberry juice

Vermouth or Grande Marnier

Lemon pieces

Sugar (to taste) & Ice cubes.

If you are having this cocktail before lunch make it using Vermouth. If you are taking it after lunch, swap the Vermouth for Grande Marnier.

PACHARÁN

Made from sloe berries (endrinas) much in the manner we would make sloe gin, but replacing the gin with anís or orujo. Put enough sloe berries into a bottle until it is one quarter full. Fill to the brim with sweet anís or orujo. Add 4 coffee beans and a cinnamon stick and seal and store for six months. Filter and serve with ice.

The best pre-bottled variety of Pacharán is from the Spanish province of Navarra. It is a great alternative to after-dinner chupitos as it is less strong.

PEDRO XIMÉNEZ

A real treat for sweet sherry lovers. This sherry is dark, and rich with a bouquet of raisins made from sun-dried Pedro Ximénez grapes, a variety that has been grown on the southern slopes of Andalusia for centuries.

'Pedro Ximen ' is a Spanish translation from the original Arab grape variety which, in English, translates as 'The golden drop'.

It is a great accompaniment to drink with dessert.

YOUR ROUND/MY ROUND: MEMORY

A drinkers lifestyle can irritate haemarrhoids or piles. No laughing matter. You can make it one by betting your drinking buddies on the eight ways of saying "piles" in cockney rhyming slang, for the next round. Here goes:

Cockneys in Benidorm can be heard complaining about their "Metrics" (Miles), "Ziggies" (Sieg Heils) and "Dukes" (of Argylles), as in "My Dukes are giving me jip". Add "Nuremburgs" (Trials) "Farmers" (Giles), "Nobbies" (Stiles), Rockfords" (Files) and "Chalfont's" (St. Giles) and there you have it.

(ANSWERS P79)

PONCHE

Ponche comes in a very distinct chromed bottle. The most popular being Ponche Caballero. In English the word means 'punch'.

Ponche consists of Spanish brandy mixed with extract of orange peel, fruits and spices and weighs in at around 27º proof, so it also packs a punch.

For a long drink, mix it with fruit juice, soda or milk, with ice.

THE THINGS THEY SAY

"I've formed a group called Alcoholics- Unanimous. If you don't feel like a drink, you ring another member and he comes over to persuade you."

Richard Harris

RON

Rum is a the most popular cocktail base in Spain. Try a Mojito, a Cuban cocktail made with rum, brown sugar, mint, lime-juice and sparkling water.

Most people associate Havana Club as the best Cuban rum, but whilst you're in Spain grab the chance to try the Matusalem, 15-year old rum from Venezuela.

'Ron y Miel' is rum blended with honey. 'Arehucas' is a smooth flavoured brand from the Canary Islands.

SANGRIA

Sangria is a refreshing summer drink. Recipes vary but this is a good one.

1 litre of red wine, 1 tablespoon of sugar,
The juice of one orange,
Half a litre of club soda (use 'Casera'),
Slices of orange, lemon and peach,
A stick of cinnamon.

Brandy or Cointreau can be added to get it up on its feet. Best left to chill overnight in the fridge, then serve with ice.

SOBREMESA

In Spain you don't have to leave your table just because you've finished eating. Cheaper restaurants may pressure you to give-up your table as they rely on more covers at lunchtime. Better to relax.

The Sobremesa is a great over-the-table laugh or discussion and the ideal way to digest your food after a good lunch. It can go on for hours and often sounds like an argument. This is because it is usually fuelled by the rounds of spirits or cocktails that go with it.

SPANISH CAVA COCKTAIL

A cocktail from the orange growing region of Valencia.

Mix one bottle of Spanish Cava with 1 litre of fresh orange juice (and it must be fresh!).

Add Cointreau to taste and serve over ice cubes.

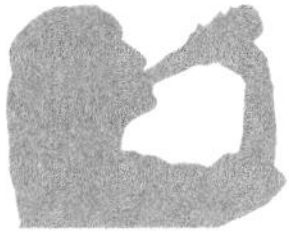

Ask Beni: Drunk is ugly. Keep drinking happy

HOLIDAY BOOK 2

"A wave of unsteady pleasure, like a flutter of ruffling wind across the water on a summer afternoon, ran through Mr Charlton's veins and set them dancing. He drank again. He felt a sudden lively and uncontrollable desire to pick strawberries on warm misdsummer evenings, no matter what happened.

"My God, this is great stuff", he told everybody."

'The Darling Buds of May' by H.E. Bates

(extract: courtesy of Pollinger)

THE THINGS THEY SAY

"Two great European narcotics, alcohol and Christianity."

Friedrich Nietzsche.

SOL Y SOMBRA

One to start the day with a bang.

Sol y Sombra means 'sun and shade', and refers to the double layer of anís and brandy in this traditional Andalusian agricultural worker's wake-up tonic. It is usually served in a small brandy glass called a brandy snifter.

There is an alternative cocktail version of Sol y Sombra which is a shaken mixture of Spanish brandy and gin poured over crushed ice.

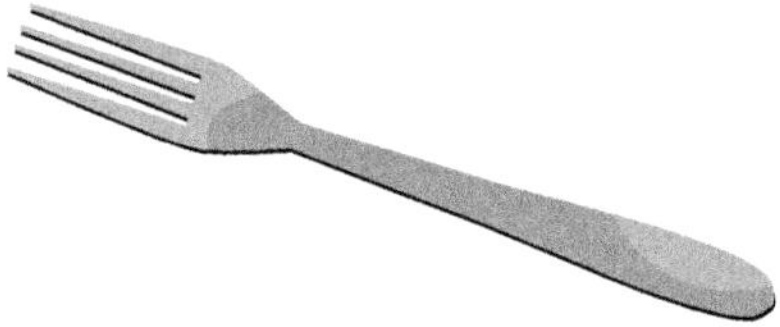

TAPAS

Around 1810, due to the amount of drunkeness among his troops, Pepe Botella (Napoleon's brother) in his short reign as José I of Spain, brought in a law that obliged bar owners to provide a bite-sized portion of food with each alcoholic drink. This was placed on top of the drink to keep the flies off, and the Tapa (which means 'lid') was born.

The tradition continues in many Spanish regions and in Granada they are fabulous. Although, tapas are still free, you often get what you're given, which is not always what you want.

TINTO DE VERANO

Verano means summer, and this mix of red table wine and Casera (sugar-free lemonade) over ice, is a popular and refreshing summer drink. Think of it as the Spanish version of our Spritzer (white wine and soda). The proportions of wine to lemonade vary.

Red table wine has always been, not just a drink with lunch, but an essential part of the lunchtime 'menú' in Spain. Nowadays, Tinto de Verano using plenty of Casera is commonly chosen with a menu, due to the basic quality of the wine on offer and the pressures of drink-driving.

VERMUT

Vermut (Vermouth) is wine infused with herbs, sugar, caramel and water. The most popular Spanish Vermouth comes from Reus in Tarragona and can be found on draft tap in many bars.

There are three types. Dry vermouth which is white, sweet vermouth which is white (bianco) or red vermouth (rosso).

There are over 200 Vermouth based cocktails often drunk as appetizers before lunch.

YOUR ROUND / MY ROUND: FACTFILE

TRUE OR FALSE: Benidorm's beaches have only ever been blue flag beaches.

TRUE OR FALSE: Benidorm has an all-weather cricket pitch with a grass outfield.

TRUE OR FALSE: Benidorm is Europe's third largest tourist resort after London & Paris.

(ANSWERS P79)

THE THINGS THEY SAY

"Con pan y vino se anda el camino." With bread and wine you can follow your path. - ***Spanish proverb***

VINO

Wine is a drink made from grapes fermented in barrels. That may sound obvious but, to the Spanish, there is no such thing as other-fruit wines. Wine includes sherries and cavas as well as red, white and rosé wines but it does not include elderberries.

Spain has nothing to prove. The country has been producing wine for over 2000 years and has more acres of vineyard than any other country in the world. Here are some basics to help you choose a good one.

AGE OF WINES:

COSECHA, CRIANZA, RESERVA AND GRAN RESERVA

Wine from last year's harvest is called 'Cosecha'. Much better quality are 'Crianzas', wine that is at least 2 years old, 6 months in the barrel and 18 months bottled. Reserva wines are more than 2 years old for white and rosé wines, and 4 years old for red wines. Gran Reserva red wines are over 5 years old with a minimum 24 months in the barrel and 36 months bottled.

VINO TINTO

Red Wine. The two outstanding wine growing regions in Spain are Ribera del Duero, home of Spain's most sought after wine Vega Sicilia, and La Rioja. La Rioja has three wine producing areas: Alta, Baja and Alavesa. Rioja wines made their mark in the 1970's as a good substitute for more expensive French clarets and the region now has a reputation for excellence. Another highly valued wine is Priorato from Catalonia.

If you like sweet reds, journey south in your search and try wines from Malaga in Andalusia.

OTHER RED WINES

Spain boasts 56 quality controlled wine regions known as Denominaciónes de Orígen (look for 'D.O.' on the wine label). Red wines from Toro, Madrid and León are well worth trying, for their traditional grape varieties.

Wines from La Mancha, Valdapeñas and Benidorm's own region, Levante (Valencia, Alicante and Utiel-Requena wines) now boast better bottling technology and have finally broken away from the poor reputation they had in the UK in the 1970's.

VINO BLANCO

White wine. Quality Spanish white wines are produced using local grapes. The best whites are from Rías Baixas in Galicia. Here, the Albariño grape produces a crisp, delicate wine.

The best Rueda white wine from Valladolid region are made using the Verdejo grape which produces a fruity white full of flavour.

If you like sweet, dessert white wines try Ochoa from Navarra.

OTHER WHITE WINES

Txakolin (pronounced "chacolee") is very refreshing and easy to drink, young white wine produced from green, fruity grapes in the Basque country. It is slightly fizzy and light and between 10'5-11,5^{o} proof.

For stronger flavours try the award-winning whites from Montilla-Moriles near Cordoba, Andalusia. These are strong and, in most cases un-fortified. The constant warm weather ensures the grapes have a high sugar content and therefore there is a higher natural alcohol content in the finished wine.

VINO ROSÉ

Look no further than wines from Navarra. With only a few wineries producing reds and whites, Navarra has long lived in the shadow of its better known wine producing neighbour, La Rioja. Today, Navarra stands out as Spains best region for good value and quality Rosé wines.

The main wineries are: Sarria, Guelbenzu, Irache, Chivite &, Ochoa. If you are passing through Navarra be on the look out for small wine producers that sell fresh Rosé wines without a label.

YOUR ROUND / MY ROUND: YOUR CHOICE

1. High season how many lifeguards are on Benidorm's beaches? a) 10-20 b) 20-30 c) 30-40

2. Benidorm is on the same line of longitude as:
a) Cambridge b) Moscow c) Paris

3. British runners in the Benidorm marathon make up: a) 30-40% b) 40-50% c) 50-60%

(ANSWERS P79)

THE THINGS THEY SAY

"I'd rather have a free bottle in front of me than a pre-frontal lobotomy."

Tom Waits, Musician

HANGOVER CURES

You feel like you've been sucking on a badger's bottom. Your brain has shrunk to the size of a walnut. The toxins your liver produced processing the alcohol, are winding you up and getting you down, and the booze you hosed down a wall last night has flushed essential vitamins and minerals from your body. A hair of the dog may steady your nerves but a hangover's going to happen sooner or later. Let's ease the pain.

A BLOODY MARY

The Tabasco will get your system fired up and sweat out the alcohol toxins. The vodka will soften the blow. The tomato juice and celery will give you vitamins and minerals, and with ice, make you less thirsty. Worcestershire sauce adds the magic that should take effect about 20 minutes later.

Three parts Tomato juice,

One part vodka

Four teaspoons Worcestershire sauce,

Three drops of Tabasco sauce A celery stick

CARRY ON JEEVES

In the book 'Carry On Jeeves' by P.G. Wodehouse, the toff Bertie Wooster takes on his new butler after being saved by Jeeves's hangover cure.

"It is a little preparation of my own invention," says Jeeves, "It is the Worcestershire sauce that gives it its colour. The raw egg makes it nutritious. The red pepper (chile pepper) gives it its bite."

Over to you.

COKE, COFFEE OR FRUIT JUICE

All these drinks help make your hangover a less thirsty experience.

The fizz in Coke will make you feel less like vomiting. The caffeine and sugar-hit in Coke and coffee will make you feel more lively.

Fruit juices are a healthier first choice alternative. Whether you drink juices or a glass of water, wash down a Vitamin C tablet at the same time.

COLD CHOCOLATE MILK

Chocolate milk will soothe and coat your stomach to stop you feeling sick. Chocolate also replaces some of the vitamins your body has lost. The sugars (lactose and sucrose) in the drink are a source of new energy that your overworked liver can still process.

Chocolate is also known to help against the effects of mild depression, and we all know how good it tastes.

THE THINGS THEY SAY

"If you take a mouse, lock it up in a cage with barely enough room to turn around, deprive it of environmental stimulus, meaningful activity, social intercourse or any hope of escape other than death and then offer it drugs: the mouse will intoxicate itself to extinction."

Grugyn Silverbristle.

THE DUTCH CURE

Scientists in Amsterdam investigating withdrawal symptoms from substance abuse discovered that the following ingredients when taken together, stimulate the production of seratonin, the naturally occuring chemical in the body that gives people a feeling of well-being.

2 tablets of folic acid

1 vitamin B complex tablet

1 packet of cashew nuts

2 bananas

MARMITE ON COLD PIZZA

Some food in your stomach is good, but something salty is better. A pizza base also has fibres in it which prevent water in the topping from seeping through to the cooked dough, so cold pizza doesn't go soggy.

As fat and water don't mix, the tomato puree keeps the melted cheese away from the base, so the next day it is less oily and easier to digest.

You get Vitamin B from the Marmite.

SAUERKRAUT

Eating cabbage to cure a hangover goes back hundreds of years. Sauerkraut is an East European dish of stewed cabbage and onions with sugar and salt to taste.

Beer-swilling Germans are big on this. They eat it to halt the hangover process, balance stomach acids and for a source of vitamins and sugar. You can also drink the juice on its own. It tastes foul but works wonders.

FRIED BREAKFAST WITH A MILKSHAKE

Eggs, bacon, tomato, mushrooms, sausage and toast is high on calories but works like a charm for most Brits.

The grease from the bacon and sausage coats the stomach and replaces minerals. The tomato replaces vitamins. As an alternative to lashings of tea, which gives you well-needed liquid, a milkshake is the magic touch that will calm your stomach and relax you.

LEFT-OVER CURRY

Spices like clove oil, ginger and garlic used in curry recipes are essential oils which help digestion. Oils and spices that sit overnight in a left-over curry also continue working on the meat to make it more tender. The smell from a curry acts like aromatherapy to help calm your over-stressed system and any left-over rice will soak up some of the excess acid in your stomach.

PILLS

There are hangover pills you can buy, but any pill you swallow will probably make you sick. Don't take them just before going to bed. Paracetamol and Aspirin are strong on an already fragile liver and stomach. Tylenol damages your liver as much as alcohol does. Ibuprofen might help. It's your choice, but far better to limit pill taking to supplements. Vitamin C can be taken to replace this vitamin lost from your system when you were on the booze.

EXERCISE

In Britain, 7 out of 10 people are physically, emotionally or nutritionally unfit. If you are unfit it is difficult to cope with a hangover. It is also true that obesity, osteoporosis and heart disease are health risk factors that increase if you drink. So your holiday is the ideal time to up the ante on exercise in a way that suits you. Swim every day, relax big time, and enjoy plenty of high-octane sex. All great for increasing fitness and coping with a holiday sized hangover.

THE THINGS THEY SAY

"I feel sorry for people who don't drink. They wake up in the morning and that's the best they're gonna feel all day!"

Jim McLean 1928-2005

QUICKFIRE EXCUSES

Need to get off the beach and into the pub? Came home late? (it doesn't matter how late). Smell like a brewery? Stains on your shirt? Never answered your mobile? Lost a shoe?

Here are some quickfire excuses that will get you out of trouble, or alternatively, deeper into it. Tips to smooth over those holiday wrinkles that were not made by too much sun, but by too much booze.

GETTING OFF THE BEACH & INTO THE PUB

The Jellyfish method. Bite your knee, then tell your partner you think you've been stung by a Jellyfish. It is important you get to the chemist before it closes to buy antihistamine cream. Better to do this than see the lifeguard because you also need a postcard for your Mum and so can pick one up on the way. You also need the bathroom and can't go for a wee in the sea because you are paranoid about jellyfish. Finally, casually mention as you leave, that you've dodgy coverage on your mobile phone.

DIDN'T MAKE IT HOME LAST NIGHT

Wait for the shops to open. Buy a souvenir of Madrid. Make sure the souvenir isn't heavy as it may get thrown back in your face. When you get back to your hotel, tell your partner the taxi went the wrong way. If you can't remember the name of your hotel, write it on your knee. That way, as you try to get up off the pavement having failed to grab hold of the taxi door, it will gradually come into focus.

YOU SMELL LIKE A BREWERY

Beer shower gel replaces the sweaty smell of beer with a soapy, clean smell of beer. Splash on cologne Alvarez Gomez. This is a famous spanish gentlemen's cologne from Seville that has a dignified lemon smell. Use Clorohexadina mouth wash but be careful not to drop your chewing gum on your way out, as you now smell like a "tart's boudoir", and may get a bigger surprise than you bargained for as you bend over to pick it up.

TELL-TALE STAINS ON YOUR T-SHIRT

Before the shops close buy a spray bottle of "Quita Manchas" (stain-remover). Hide it amongst the rocks on the shoreline. Check the tide isn't coming in. When it's time to stagger home, recover the bottle and spray on your t-shirt stains. Don't drink the rest of the bottle. Rinse your t-shirt off in the sea and spread out flat on a rock. Go for a head-clearing swim whilst it dries in the sun before going back to the hotel to face the music.

FAILED TO HEAR YOUR MOBILE PHONE

No coverage? Run out of battery? A likely story. Better to say Demaria Leyton (yes, Sticky Vicky's daughter) borrowed it for her act and you couldn't get it back until she'd juggled it with twelve ping-pong balls, five light bulbs and several pieces of period furniture. After a couple of hours it was returned, but curiously, you couldn't pick up coverage, until just after the football finished on satellite TV.

LOST YOUR SHOE

Throw away your other shoe and walk back to the hotel barefoot. Tell your partner you've renounced alcohol, turned to Jesus and spent the entire night reading the Bible.

The Benidorm Boozer's Bible, naturally...

Check out - The Tree of Dissipation -The Reverand Gooch, The Victoria Gem (1843)

ANSWERS: YOUR ROUND, MY ROUND

p.25 STATS - TRUE OR FALSE:
1. True, 2. Not any more, 3. True

p.34 8 NAMES FOR PILES:
Metrics, Ziggies, Dukes, Farmers, Nobbies, Nurembergs, Rockfords, Chalfonts.

p.47 FACTFILE - TRUE OR FALSE:
1.True – an eco-label for top quality
2.False – it's in Albir
3.True

p.56 YOUR CHOICE:
1. c) 34 lifeguards
2. a) Cambridge
3. c) Over 50%

LEGAL

Only try what you are able to try. Use good sense and consume alcoholic drinks in moderation.

'THE BENIDORM BOOZER'S BIBLE'

iainmclean2.wixsite.com/boozersbible

Printed in Dunstable, United Kingdom

75496020R00047